Table of Contents

....	1
Introduction	3
Cocodas	4
Mexican Brownies	6
Fried Ice Cream	8
Elephant Ears	10
Bananas Foster	12
Dulche Du Leche	14
Cadillac Margarita	16
Strawberry Agua Fresca	18
Snow Cone Syrup	20
Sopapilla Martini	22
Chamango	24
Mexican Hot Chocolate	26
Crispy Onion Rings	28
Vanilla Chia Dessert	30
Sopapillas	32
4 ingredient Quesadilla	34
Hot Fudge Sundae	36
Mexican Choco Tofu Pudding	38
Groovy Banana Blitz	40
Champurrado	42
Mexican Chocolate Shot	44
Mangonada	46
Pecan Balls	48
Carlota de Limon	50
Bionicos	52
Fresas Con Crema	54
Churro	56
Mexican Fruit Cocktail	58
Fruit Empanadas	60
Impossible Cake	62
Conclusion	64

Like Water of Chocolate - Classic Mexican Desserts you will love

Mexican desserts you can't say No!!

BY: Ida Smith

Copyright © 2021 by Ida Smith. All Rights Reserved.

License Notes

This book is licensed for your personal enjoyment only. This book may not be re-sold or given away to other people. If you would like to share this book with another person, please purchase an additional copy for each recipient. If you're reading this book and did not purchase it, or it was not purchased for your use only, then please return to your favorite ebook retailer and purchase your own copy. Thank you for respecting the hard work of this author.

Introduction

This cookbook doesn't only celebrate the deliciousness and awesomeness of Mexican desserts, but it also celebrates the durability and agelessness of them as they are being transferred from one generation to another.

In celebrating, the 30 dessert recipes are yours to explore!!!

Cocodas

Chewy, delicious and soft, these are coconut candies that you wouldn't want to share with anyone!!!

Preparation Time: 10 minutes
Cooking time: 13 minutes
Yield: 15
Ingredient List:

- 3 ounces chopped macadamia nuts
- 15 ounces Dulce de leche
- 6 cups shredded coconut

Preparation:
Preheat your oven to 348 degrees F.

Place parchment paper on a baking sheet to line it. Mix the Dulce de Leche, coconut, and nuts in a bowl.

Scoop out 15 pieces and arrange them on a cookie sheet.

Bake for 13 minutes till golden.

Cool and serve.

Mexican Brownies

These are the brownies we can vouch for!!!
Preparation Time: 10 minutes
Cooking time: 15 minutes
Yield: 10
Ingredient List:

- 1 cup sugar
- 1 stick soft butter
- 2 eggs
- 8 tablespoons flour
- 1 teaspoon vanilla extract
- 9 tablespoons cocoa powder
- 1 pinch cinnamon

- 1 sprinkle baking powder
- 1 pinch salt
- 1 pinch cayenne paper

Preparation:
Preheat the oven to 348 degrees F.
Cover a baking dish with parchment.
Grease the paper lightly with butter.
Put the butter, vanilla, sugar, and eggs in a bowl. Mix well.
Toss in the salt, chili, cinnamon, flour, and cocoa. Mix well.
Pour and spread the mixture into the pan.
Bake for 20 minutes.
Allow to cooling.
Serve.

Fried Ice Cream

It sounds out of the world, right? So does it taste!!!
Preparation Time: 07 minutes
Cooking time: 04 minutes
Yield: 4
Ingredient List:

- 16 ounces vanilla ice cream
- 2 egg whites (beaten)
- 2 cups cornflakes (crushed)
- 1 quart oil

Preparation:
Scoop and arrange the Ice cream into balls on a baking sheet.

Mix the cinnamon and cornflakes in a bowl.
Coat the ice cream balls in the mixture and the egg white.
Chill the coated balls for 2 hours.
Fry the ice cream balls in oil.
Drain and serve.

Elephant Ears

Not what you think it is!!!

Preparation Time: 10 minutes
Cooking time: 15 minutes
Yield: 10
Ingredient List:

- 1 pinch salt
- 8 tablespoons sugar (divided)
- 1 pinch cinnamon
- 1 sheet defrosted puff pastry

Preparation:
Preheat the oven to 452 degrees.

Put 4 tablespoons of sugar and the salt in a bowl. Mix well.
Pour the mixture on a board.
Spread the puff pastry in the mixture.
Put the cinnamon and 4 tablespoons of sugar in a bowl.
Spread on the puff pastry.
Roll the puff pastry into a square (13 inches).
Fold the square sides so that the two ends meet in the middle.
Fold one half of the dough over the other half of the dough.
Slice the dough and arrange the slices in a baking sheet that you have lined with parchment paper.
Bake till caramelized. Transfer to cool on a rake.
Serve.

Bananas Foster

Not only is this Mexican dessert delicious, but it's also a classic that dates back to the 1950s!!!

Preparation Time: 04 minutes
Cooking time: 08 minutes
Yield: 2
Ingredient List:

- 2 sliced ripe bananas (cut lengthwise)
- 1 teaspoon cinnamon
- 1 tablespoon vanilla
- 8 ounces ice cream (vanilla)
- 2 tablespoons bourbon
- 2 tablespoons butter
- 2 tablespoons chopped pecans

- 4 tablespoons sugar (dark brown)
- 2 tablespoons banana liqueur

Preparation:
Put the butter and sugar in a pan.
Melt the butter.
Toss in the cinnamon, pecans, and vanilla. Stir well.
Place the bananas in the sauce. Continue to heat till they are soft.
Put off the heat.
Pour in the bourbon and banana liqueur. Light the sauce with a lighter.
When the fire subsides, serve and top with the ice cream.

Dulche Du Leche

Just stir!!!

Preparation Time: 25 minutes
Cooking time: 1 hour
Yield: 1
Ingredient List:

- 1 pinch vanilla
- 10 tablespoons sugar
- 2 cups milk
- 1 pinch baking soda
- 7 ounces condensed milk

Preparation:

Put the milk, baking soda, and sugar in a saucepan.
Stir well. Allow simmering for 1 hour to caramelize the milk.
Allow cooling. Serve.

Cadillac Margarita

If you want to enjoy a smooth and citrusy taste of classic margarita, you can do no wrong with this recipe!!

Preparation Time: 03 minutes
Cooking time: nil
Yield: 1
Ingredient List:

- 1 handful ice cubes
- 1 ounce syrup
- 2 ounces tequila
- 1 ounce Grand Marnier
- 2 ounces lemon juice
- 1 orange wedge

Preparation:
Put the ice in a glass.
Toss in the syrup, lemon juice, and tequila. Mix.
Top with the tequila. Mix well.
Garnish with the orange wedge.

Strawberry Agua Fresca

For the love of strawberry!!!
Preparation Time: 05 minutes
Cooking time: nil
Yield: 3
Ingredient List:

- 2 cups hulled strawberry
- 2 cups water
- 1 squeezed lemon
- 3 tablespoons sugar

Preparation:
Dissolve the sugar in water.

Blend the strawberries till smooth.
Put the mixture, the sugar mixture, and lemon juice in a bowl.
Stir well.
Serve.

Snow Cone Syrup

Yummy!!!

Preparation Time: 03 minutes
Cooking time: 01 minute
Yield: 5
Ingredient List:

- 1 cup sugar (white)
- 1 ounce soft drink (fruit flavor)
- 8 tablespoons water

Preparation:
Boil the water and sugar in a pan for one minute.
Turn off the heat.

Add in the fruit flavor. Mix well.
Allow cooling before pouring into a glass of shaved ice.

Sopapilla Martini

This martini is so rich and delicious that you won't mind boycotting your food desserts for it.

Preparation Time: 10 minutes
Cooking time: nil
Yield: 1
Ingredient List:

- 1 ounce martini
- 2 ounces honey syrup
- 1 teaspoon cinnamon
- 2 drops honey
- 1 ounce vodka
- 1 handful soft cashews
- 2 ounces spiced rum
- 1 pinch cinnamon sugar

– 1 cinnamon stick

Preparation:
Spread the honey on a plate.
Spread the cinnamon sugar on another plate.
Coat the rim of the glass with the honey and cinnamon.
Set the glass aside.
Blend the cashew, vodka, cinnamon, rum, and honey syrup.
Sieve the mixture into the glass.
Garnish with the cinnamon stick.
Enjoy.

Chamango

All you need to get hooked is a single taste of it!!

Preparation Time: 07 minutes
Cooking time: nil
Yield: 1
Ingredient List:

- 1 cup chamoy
- 1 apricot
- 1 handful ice cube
- 1 handful diced tamarind candy
- 1 cup diced mangoes

Preparation:

Blend a larger part of the mango and ice.
Fill your glass with the remaining mango pieces.
Add 2 tablespoons of chamoy.
Add 4 tablespoons of the mango mixture.
Add another layer of the mango pieces.
And more chamoy.
And mango mixture.
And more chamoy, mango pieces, and tamarind candy to top it.
Enjoy.

Mexican Hot Chocolate

Something delicious and spicy for winter!!!
Preparation Time: 03 minutes
Cooking time: 06 minutes
Yield: 2
Ingredient List:

- 2 ounces bittersweet chocolate
- 1 teaspoon vanilla extract
- 3 tablespoons sugar (granulated)
- 3 cups milk
- 1 teaspoon ground cinnamon
- 3 tablespoons cocoa powder (unsweetened)
- 1 pinch chili powder

– 1 pinch cayenne pepper

Preparation:
Cook the ingredients in a pan.
Stir till the chocolate melts and the mixture is boiling.
Serve.
Enjoy.

Crispy Onion Rings

How to snack on onions only!!!!

Preparation Time: 10 minutes
Cooking time: 10 minutes
Yield: 20
Ingredient List:

- 2 beaten eggs
- 2 large-sized sweet onions (sliced thick)
- 1 pinch salt
- 7 tablespoons almond flour
- 1 pinch pepper
- 6 tablespoons cheese (parmesan)
- 1 pinch parsley

- 2 tablespoons coconut flour
- 2 cups oil
- 1 pinch paprika

Preparation:
Mix the spices, cheese, and flours in a bowl.
Toss the onions inside the bowl of egg first.
Then in the flour mixture.
Then again in the egg.
And again in the flour mixture.
Fry the onions in a pan of hot oil till Crispy.
Drain the onions and serve.

Vanilla Chia Dessert

Either as a snack, side meal, or dessert, this serving of creamy goodness is here to cater to your need!!

Preparation Time: 07 minutes
Cooking time: nil
Yield: 2
Ingredient List:

- 2 handfuls chia seeds
- 1 tablespoon coconut syrup
- 1 tablespoon vanilla extract
- 1 cup almond milk

Preparation:
Mix the coconut syrup, chia seeds, vanilla, and almond milk in a bowl.

Mix well till the seeds sink.
Chill for a while and serve.

Sopapillas

This Sopapillas recipe will make you say bye-bye to the restaurant version!!!

Preparation Time: 15 minutes
Cooking time: 10 minutes
Yield: 10
Ingredient List:

- 1 teaspoon baking powder
- 1 cup flour
- 10 tablespoons warm water
- 1 tablespoon cinnamon sugar
- 1 pinch salt
- 2 cups oil
- 1 tablespoon coconut oil

Preparation:
Put the salt, coconut oil, baking powder, and flour in a bowl. Mix well.
Slowly stir in the water to make a rough dough.
With your bare hands, knead the dough.
Shape the dough into a ball before rolling it out.
Use a rolling pin to roll out the dough before cutting it into squares.
Fry the squares till they bubble up and are golden.
Transfer to a paper-lined tray.
Serve with a sprinkle of cinnamon sugar.

4 ingredient Quesadilla

Whip up tortilla, cheese, pepper, and other ingredients to get the best Mexican Quesadilla you can ever taste!!

Preparation Time: 10 minutes
Cooking time: 20 minutes
Yield: 2
Ingredient List:

- 1 cup rinsed pinto beans (cooked and drained)
- 1 handful chopped green onion
- 1 tablespoon olive oil
- 1 handful chopped cherry tomatoes (roasted)
- 1 handful pickled jalapeño (chopped)
- 1 cup cheddar cheese (grated)

- 2 warm flour tortillas (wholegrain)

Preparation:
Sprinkle a large part of the cheese on one half of each of the flour tortilla.
Top the cheese with the onion, beans, jalapeño, and pepper.
Sprinkle the rest of the cheese over the ingredients.
Fold the unfilled side of the tortillas.
Brush the quesadillas with the oil.
Cook the quesadillas on a skillet till they are crispy on both sides.
Serve and enjoy.

Hot Fudge Sundae

We know you have never had a spicy and hot sundae, and that's why we are introducing you to this Mexican sundae!!!

Preparation Time: 08 minutes
Cooking time: nil
Yield: 1
Ingredient List:

- 4 tablespoons heavy cream (boiled)
- 3 tablespoons sweetened flaked coconut (toasted)
- 1 dash salt
- 1 pinch cinnamon
- 2 ounces chopped chocolate
- 3 scoops ice cream (chocolate)

- 1 chocolate wafer roll
- 2 tablespoons sliced almonds
- 2 tablespoons whipped cream
- 1 ounce chili nut

Preparation:
Add the salt, cinnamon, heavy cream, and chopped chocolate in a bowl. Whisk well till smooth and shiny.

Serve the ice cream in a serving bowl.

Add the cinnamon mixture on top.

Followed by coconut flakes, wafer, nuts, whipped cream, and almonds.

Enjoy.

Mexican Choco Tofu Pudding

We know tofu is not the best of ingredients, but with a touch of chocolate and sugar, your tofu meal will come out just fine!!!

Preparation Time: 10 minutes
Cooking time: 05 minutes
Yield: 4
Ingredient List:

- 1 pinch vanilla extract
- 4 ounces melted semisweet chocolate
- 1 tablespoon ground cinnamon
- 6 tablespoons sugar syrup
- 1 pinch chili powder
- 1 pound tofu (silken)

− 2 handfuls chocolate shavings

Preparation:
Put the sugar syrup and the other ingredients in a blender, except the chocolate.
Blend well.
Serve and garnish with the chocolate shavings.
Enjoy.

Groovy Banana Blitz

Let's tie and dye some smoothies!!!

Preparation Time: 07 minutes
Cooking time: nil
Yield: 1
Ingredient List:

- 1 teaspoon sugar
- 1 ripe chopped banana
- 3 ounces vanilla yogurt
- 1 cup ice
- 1 pinch different food colors and egg dyes
- 1 pinch orange extract

Preparation:
Blend the yogurt, banana, sugar, extract, and ice smoothly.
Serve the mixture into a glass.
Drop the food colors inside the glass.
Serve.

Champurrado

From generations to generations, this Mexican corn delicacy is a bomber!!!

Preparation Time: 05 minutes
Cooking time: 15 minutes
Yield: 3
Ingredient List:

- 1 pinch salt
- 2 cups milk
- 2 ounces Mexican chocolate
- 5 tablespoons Masa Harina
- 1 tablespoon sugar (brown)
- 1 pinch cinnamon

Preparation:
Put the Masa Harina, salt, and warm water in a pan.
Stir well to avoid lumping.
Toss in the milk, cinnamon, chocolate, and sugar.
Stir well to simmer.
Serve.

Mexican Chocolate Shot

Chocola – Tini!!!!

Preparation Time: 05 minutes
Cooking time: nil
Yield: 1
Ingredient List:

- 1 pinch cinnamon
- 2 tablespoons chocolate whipped cream
- 1 teaspoon amaretto
- 1 tablespoon chocolate liqueur
- 1 teaspoon vodka

Preparation:
Mix the liqueur, vodka, and Amaretto. Stir well.
Add the cream and cinnamon.

Mangonada

What better way to dazzle your palate and also cool your throat on a hot sunny day than a glass of this delicious Mango delicacy!!!

Preparation Time: 03 minutes
Cooking time: 05 minutes
Yield: 1
Ingredient List:

- 1 cup chopped mango
- 1 handful ice cube
- 1 cup mango juice
- 1 tamarind straw
- 1 teaspoon tajin
- 1 tablespoon chamoy

Preparation:
Blend the mango juice, a large portion of the mango, and the ice cubes smoothly.
Coat the rim of the glass with the chamoy and tajin.
Throw in the blended mixture into the glass.
Top with the remaining chopped mango and tamarind straw.

Pecan Balls

Pecan lovers, you are going to love this!!!
Preparation Time: 10 minutes
Cooking time: 13 minutes
Yield: 2
Ingredient List:

- 1 stick soft butter
- 1 cup flour
- 1 pinch salt
- 1 cup sugar
- 1 pinch nutmeg
- 1 teaspoon vanilla extract
- 1 cup chopped pecans

Preparation:

Preheat the oven to 351 degrees F.
Mix the butter, nutmeg, sugar, pecans, flour, salt, and vanilla in a blender.
Shape the mixture into one inch sized balls.
Arrange the balls on baking sheets.
Bake for 13 minutes.
Roll the baked balls in sugar.
Serve.

Carlota de Limon

This creamy and delicious classic Mexican no-bake cake will make you ask for more!!

Preparation Time: 15 minutes
Cooking time: nil
Yield: 3
Ingredient List:

- 4 ounces cream cheese pack
- 1 can evaporated milk
- 1 pinch ground cinnamon
- 1 can condensed milk
- 1 cup honey nut cheerios
- 4 tablespoons lime juice

Preparation:
Blend the different types of milk, lime juice, and cheese.
Put some cheerios at the bottom of the 3 dessert glasses.
Scoop in the lime mix.
Spread it to cover the cheerio.
Continue with another layer of cheerios.
And followed by the lime mix
Cover the glasses and chill for 2 hours.
Serve with a sprinkle of cinnamon.

Bionicos

Form Jalisco with love since the 90s!!!

Preparation Time: 01 minute
Cooking time: nil
Yield: 2
Ingredient List:

- 2 cups fruits (pineapple, papaya, cantaloupe, and berries)
- 2 tablespoons yogurt
- 2 tablespoons sour cream
- 2 tablespoons condensed milk
- 1 handful chopped pecans
- 1 pinch vanilla
- 2 handfuls raisins

- 1 handful granola
- 1 handful shredded coconut

Preparation:
Mix the liquid ingredients and vanilla in a bowl.
Spoon a large part of this mixture into the serving bowls.
Top with the fruits.
Spoon in the remaining vanilla mixture on the fruits.
Top with the raisin, coconut, granola, and pecans.
Enjoy.

Fresas Con Crema

Super yummy!!!
Preparation Time: 08 minutes
Cooking time: nil
Yield: 4
Ingredient List:

- 10 tablespoons sweet condescend milk
- 16 ounces hulled strawberry (sliced)
- 10 tablespoons evaporated milk
- 1 pinch vanilla extract
- 8 ounces sour cream
- 10 tablespoons heavy whipping cream

Preparation:
Put the heavy cream, milk, evaporated milk, and vanilla in a bowl.
Mix well.
Spoon the strawberry into the cups.
Top with the milk mixture.
Serve.

Churro

These are the fritters you can't resist!!!!
Preparation Time: 10 minutes
Cooking time: 10 minutes
Yield: 2
Ingredient List:

- 1 pinch salt
- 8 tablespoons water
- 2 tablespoons white sugar
- 1 quart oil
- 8 tablespoons flour
- 4 tablespoons vegetable oil
- 1 pinch cinnamon

– 5 tablespoons white sugar (for coating)

Preparation:
Put the water, 1 tablespoon of oil, flour, salt, and 2 tablespoons of sugar in a pan.
Stir to boil and form a ball.
Pour the mixture into a pastry bag with a star tip.
Pour the remaining vegetable oil into a frying pan.
Pipe the dough into the frying pipe little by little
Fry and drain.
Mix the rest of the sugar and cinnamon in a bowl.
Coat the Churros in this mixture and serve.

Mexican Fruit Cocktail

You have never tasted a food salad exciting and hot like this!!!

Preparation Time: 10 minutes
Cooking time: nil
Yield: 2
Ingredient List:

- 1 pinch salt
- 1 sliced tart apple (green)
- 1 tablespoon lemon juice
- 1 handful diced seed jalapeño
- 1 tablespoon chopped cilantro
- 1 cup cubed pineapple
- 1 handful sliced onion (red)

– 1 segmented navel orange

Preparation:
Put the jalapeño, fruits, and onions in a bowl.
Add a squeeze of lemon juice over or.
Add a sprinkle of salt.
Top with the cilantro.
Mix well.
Serve.

Fruit Empanadas

Fruit and dough!!! Oh my!!!!
Preparation Time: 15 minutes
Cooking time: 13 minutes
Yield: 3
INGREDIENT LIST:

- 1 pinch sugar
- 5 tablespoons oil
- 1 cup flour
- 1 pinch cinnamon

Fruit mixture

- 1 cup fresh fruits (2 different fruits)
- 1 dash cloves
- 1 teaspoon cinnamon
- 4 tablespoons fructose
- 1 pinch nutmeg (ground)

Preparation:

Preheat the oven to 322 degrees F.

Mash your fruits and the other ingredients in the fruit mixture category.

Mix the baking powder, enough water, sugar, flour, cinnamon, and oil in a bowl to make a silky dough.

Roll out on a surface to make a thick dough.

Cut out the dough into little circles.

Scoop 2 to 3 tablespoons of this fruit mixture in a half side of the cutout dough.

Cover and seal with the other empty side.

Seal the edges using a fork.

Bake for 13 minutes.

Add a sprinkle of cinnamon sugar.

Serve.

Impossible Cake.

This is a mission impossible made POSSIBLE!!!
Preparation Time: 15 minutes
Cooking time: 50 minutes
Yield: 6
Ingredient List:

- 1 cup flour
- 2 tablespoons warm caramel sauce
- 1 pinch baking powder
- 1 pinch baking soda
- 3 tablespoons cocoa powder
- 6 tablespoons soft butter
- 6 tablespoons whole milk

- 1 egg
- 7 tablespoons white sugar
- 1 tablespoon coffee (strong brewed)

For the flan

- 7 ounces condensed milk (sweetened)
- 1 cup evaporated milk
- 2 eggs
- 1 pinch vanilla extract

Preparation:
Preheat the oven to 352 degrees F.
Apply grease in a tube pan before dusting with flour.
Fill a baking pan with water. Warm the water in the oven.
Pour the caramel sauce into the tube pan.
Mix the baking powder, baking soda, cocoa powder, and flour in a bowl.
Put the different kinds of milk, vanilla, and 2 eggs in a blender. Blend well.
Mix the butter, sugar, coffee, and 1 egg well.
Add in the milk and flour mixture.
Mix well.
Pour the mixture into the tube pan.
Top with the egg mixture.
Put the tube in the pan of water.
Bake for 50 minutes. Allow cooling, serve, and flip.

Conclusion

Meals that are termed a classic doesn't mean that they are out of culinary vogue, as some people opine. On the contrary, it actually means that they are as good as old wine, and this is what we can say about the 30 Mexican desserts!

  Not only have the desserts sojourn from one generation to another, but they also have never for once lost their richness!!

Don't miss out!

Visit the website below and you can sign up to receive emails whenever Ida Smith publishes a new book. There's no charge and no obligation.

https://books2read.com/r/B-A-LRXL-VIMLB

BOOKS 2 READ

Connecting independent readers to independent writers.

Did you love *Like Water of Chocolate - Classic Mexican Desserts you will love: Mexican desserts you can't say No!!*? Then you should read *Amazing Must-Try Fun Fest Recipes: Amazing Food Fest Recipes from around the World*[1] by Ida Smith!

Food is one thing that everybody loves, and every celebration comes with a special once in a year kind of meals. However, why wait till the time before having your special festival meals? In this cookbook, you will find 30 unique and creative festival dishes with their recipes to make them easier for you to prepare favorite meals from the comfort of your home.

---

1. https://books2read.com/u/bzgjdq
2. https://books2read.com/u/bzgjdq

www.ingramcontent.com/pod-product-compliance
Lightning Source LLC
Chambersburg PA
CBHW081019040426
42444CB00014B/3279